"I hope my dear wife is having a happier Christmas day than I am. Should I never return to her and should chance deliver this journal into her hands, she will glean from these pages that she was never far from my thoughts and my heart will beat for her to the last."

—*Louis Nusbaumer*

Death Valley, Dec. 25, 1849

THE LOST
DEATH VALLEY '49er
JOURNAL
of Louis Nusbaumer

by
George Koenig

Death Valley '49ers Inc.
1974

This book was printed with particular pride and pleasure by
The Chalfant Press
Bishop, California
whose Death Valley ties are long and deep. It was in the Inyo Independent, found-
ed by forty-niner Pleasant Arthur Chalfant, that a letter of Manly's appeared in the
issue of July 26, 1884. The continuing interest in Death Valley is also evidenced in
W. A. Chalfant's books, "Death Valley, The Facts" and "The Story of Inyo," both
providing a wealth of Death Valley area lore and legends.

To
Syble Belden
Tom Mathew
Art Walker
and all of the other '49ers
who walk the glory trail

Death Valley view photo courtesy Union Pacific Railroad; Devil's Hole, McLean Spring, courtesy of National Park Service; and 1853 view of Los Angeles courtesy of Title and Trust Company, Los Angeles. All others from George Koenig collection.

Contents

Illustrations

INTRODUCTION

> "This day some kind of mettle was found in the tail of
> the race that looks like goald, first discovered by James
> Martial, the Boss of the Mill."
> —Henry W. Bigler, January 24, 1848

From the crude sawmill of the Swiss emigre, John Sutter,* in the wilds of the American West, the word spread like wildfire to span the seven seas.

The flame flickered feebly at first. Even by the end of 1848 there were only about 5000 mining in the 10,000 square mile region encompassing the "gold fields" of California. But as the conflagration spread, over 775 vessels sailed from the eastern seaboard ports in 1849, while some 50,000 fortune seekers wended their way overland in a trail of dust that thousands more followed.

They came from cities and farms, from all walks of life. Over prairies and mountains, around Cape Horn, across the Isthmus of Panama, through Mexico, down from the Northwest Territories, up from South America, across the Pacific from Australia and China.

Fatefully the revolutionary years of 1847-48 in Europe also gave impetus to an exodus of those with little to lose and dreams of riches to be gained by the shovel and panfull.

This is the story of one of them. A true story. The story of Louis Nusbaumer, a German who left his Black Forest home to join the rush to the end of the rainbow.

---

*Actually a German, born Johann Augustus Suter, February 23, 1803, in Kandern, Grand Duchy of Baden. Coincidentally, Nusbaumer was also a native of Baden.

Louis Nusbaumer was 28 when he arrived in New York, with his wife Elizabeth,* in pre-gold rush 1847.

For over a year he eked out a living as a clerk in a jewelry store in Newark, New Jersey. But then the word of "Gold . . . in California!" was on everyone's lips. At work. In the stores. In the taverns. On the streets. "Gold! Think of it! All for the taking by those able to bend down and scoop it up!" True it might take two, three, maybe even more months to get there. And the trail wasn't easy. But to men of good health and spirit there should be no insurmountable problems. And there was· an abundance of such men to match the abundance of gold *if* they got to California early enough.

Louis and his wife talked it over. Money, carefully hoarded penny by penny, was set aside. Not only for supplies and equipment for the venture, but to sustain his beloved, and pregnant, "Lisette" until he could return with sacks of gold dust to place at her feet.

But there was also another problem. Nusbaumer spoke very little English. This meant finding a group who were also bonded by language as well as by habits and heritage. Assuredly it would make traveling more enjoyable and easier than with strangers.

So it was that some sixty compatriots organized themselves as the "German California Mining Company" and rendezvoused at the docks of New York in March of 1849.

But this was not to be a long voyage around Cape Horn. Or even to the Panamanian isthmus for a feverish trek across country to the Pacific Ocean where they might, or might not, find available passage to California.

Somewhat ironically, Nusbaumer left New York by steamer back to New Jersey and the port of South Amboy. Here a streaming and sweating mass of humanity was packed into a train with dogs, luggage and supplies. Although the trip took only a few hours it seemed an eternity of hardship. Fortunately they did not then know what yet was in store.

Interestingly, she was born in Mobile, Alabama, returning to Germany at the the age of three with her parents.

10

Then on by steamer again to Philadelphia, and again by train to Columbia and then on by canal boat ". . . where seventy men were stowed away in a room intended for thirty." Then another short haul by train, and another canal boat until they reached Pittsburg. Here they boarded river boats down the Ohio River to St. Louis. Eventually, on May 5th, they reached Independence, Missouri, the last settlement before undertaking some 1500 miles of wilderness ahead.

The Nusbaumer journal was "lost" for well over a hundred years. Clues of its existence appeared in 1941 and 1944 as brief extracts. But it was not until 1966 that the original journal was regained after a long and arduous search.

It proved to be two small, well-worn pocket notebooks. The oft faded pages were tightly written in old German script. A few pages were missing. But in view of the ravages of time it is a wonder that so much of these slim, fragile pocketbooks survived.

The tale of the Death Valley Forty-niners has been told many times. Yet its telling is as fragmented as the splintering of the parties, as clouded as memories dimmed by time. And most were later day recollections. Manly's classic account was written 40 years later.* Similarly the writings of other '49ers, including Jay-hawkers Colton, Mecum, Stephens, Clay and Shannon, as well as those of the Briers, were all recollections.

Only three accounts are known that were written on the trail as the events occurred. One is the Jayhawker Asa Haynes diary, with brief undated entries of distances and directions. Another, that of ex-sailor Sheldon Young, "logs" the travels of a small independent party that was for the most part separated from the others approaching and leaving Death Valley.

*"DEATH VALLEY IN '49", published in 1894. His first manuscript, written in 1852 from memorandum notes, was destroyed by fire. A "lost" account was reportedly dictated to a Bancroft representative. A serialized version periodically appeared in THE SANTA CLARA MONTHLY from 1887 to 1890 headed "FROM VERMONT TO CALIFORNIA". Other writings appeared from time to time in the SAN JOSE PIONEER, PACIFIC TREE & VINE, and INYO INDEPENDENT.

11

The Nusbaumer journal is the only one yet found to be brought out by the historic Bennetts-Arcanes "Long Camp" party.

Written by the flickering light of campfires and in the sparse shade of the mesquite, Nusbaumer's journal was that of a man who traveled with Manly and Rogers and watched them leave on their almost hopeless quest for help. It is the journal of a man who lost one companion as the only known '49er fatality within Death Valley, and three others whose deaths are a part of its lore and legend.

A span of 125 years disappears as he says, *"Today* one of our oxen is about to die." *"Today* is Christmas Day in the mountains of California, written in camp just before leaving."

Since they were often separated, and given to recording or recalling different occurrences in different manners, the story of Louis Nusbaumer had to be woven in with the accounts of other '49ers to corroborate times, places, names and events.

This was done by this writer, and superbly published in the Bancroft Library's "Valley of Salt, Memories of Wine." Deepfelt appreciation is gratefully asknowledged for their kind permission to publish this less academic version. Hopefully it will inspire you to use and to support the Friends of the Bancroft Library (c/o University of California, Berkeley, California 94720) to whom we are all indebted for their preservation of so much of the great wealth of our California heritage.

—George Koenig

Louis Nusbaumer, Death Valley Forty-Niner

Routes of the Death Valley wagon train and the "horse and mule"
parties from Mt. Misery across Nevada in 1849-50, superimposed on
an early 1881 map.

WAGONS, HO!

In early 1849 Independence, Missouri, was a town in name only. The streets were mud. The buildings crude. A few were of costly sawed or hauled-in lumber. Most were of logs, or tents, or a combination. The best patronized were the saloons and the supply-outfitters, with restricted stocks and unrestricted prices.

It was a town that seemingly never slept. Day and night activity reigned. Swaggering, boasting "Mountain Men," Santa Fe traders, emigrants, gold-seekers, a spattering of army men and Indians milled about in an unending stream and ceaseless turmoil.

Above the cries and curses of men, the bellowing of cattle, the clouds of dust, there hovered an air of excitement. The intoxication of adventure quickened the step and lightened the spirit. Whatever one's past, a new life lay ahead. The clerk, heretofore armed only with pen and paper, donned bowie knife and six gun. Bank president and groceryman became indistinguishable comrades. The uncertainties of what lay ahead forged a common bond. It was a time that each, whatever paths he would eventually follow, would recall nostalgically. Rarely, before or after, was there to be such a feeling of "liberty, equality, fraternity" in all of its true meaning.

It was also a time of testing the mettle of men. Towns like Independence were not only a bridge to the frontier, to an unknown future, but a bridge between men. And the testing was as much within each man as with the others on whom he was to depend and be depended upon. Indeed, the river ahead of them was more than a geographical boundary. It marked the crossing into another life.

15

So it was that, like many other groups, the German California Mining Company camped on the outskirts of this small center of civilization's frontier outpost.

There were supplies to be checked, equipment repaired and last minute needs bought, borrowed, sometimes stolen. Horses, mules, oxen, cattle had to be readied and rested for the long trail ahead. Wagons, wheels, axles inspected. Needless baggage and supplies discarded or traded.

The undertaking was not one to be taken lightly nor ill-timed To start too early, before the snow melted and grass appeared in sufficient quantity for the stock, was foolhardy. Yet to leave late hazarded forage exhausted by those who did go ahead. Not to mention getting in too late on the golden treasures half a continent away.

But with spring thaws, torrential rains came. Impatient overland travelers chafed at the reports of flooded low-lands and overflowing creeks and rivers. To cross at passably shallow fords they had to wait . . . wait . . .wait. Days and weeks passed. The emigrants whiled away the time. Some productively. Some in boredom. All gazing westerly.

Finally, after anxiously watching the skies and awaiting word and rumors, there came the joyous cry of "Wagons, ho!" And the German California Mining Company moved out with four wagons, loaded with hundreds of pounds of supplies and equipment, on the 20th of May, 1849.

A little over four months later Nusbaumer reached Salt Lake City. It had been a rather typical overland journey, with seemingly endless days of rain, parching dust and the occasional sight of Indians, antelope and buffalo. That the trek took somewhat longer than usual was due to Nusbaumer parting from his company at Fort Kearney due to constant dissension. After laying over two weeks, he arrived at Fort Laramie on August 3rd, and Salt Lake City on September 30.

Fatefully, in the late summer of 1849, at this fledgling settlement near the Great Salt Lake in the Provisional State of Deseret

16

that was to become Utah, the remnants of various wagon trains began to assemble.

It was a time and place of crucial decision. To continue westward risked a winter crossing of the Sierra Nevada and a possible repetition of the Donner tragedy in which 36 survived, many by cannabalizing some of the 45 who perished. Yet to turn back after having come so far and sacrificed so much was unthinkable. Nor could they stay in the small Morman settlement which was hard put to support its own let alone a gathering horde of emigrants.

Debates over which route to take gave way to violent arguments. Lifelong friends parted ways. Even families were divided, although sometimes motivated by an instinctive desire not to risk the loss of the entire family over one route.

Gradually the wagon trains began to break apart. Some, gambling that they could make it, went on via the Humboldt River westward. Others, reluctant to risk family and prized possessions, milled about uncertainly. Caught twixt the devil and the deep they hesitated while chilling weather heralded oncoming winter.

There was a trail, of sorts, southward. Little was known of it. But a guide was found. Captain Jefferson Hunt. He had been over the trail twice. Late in 1847 he and his two sons had been members of a Mormon party sent to secure "cattle, seed grain and fruit cuttings" from Southern California; returning in the spring of 1848. Yet strangely enough, this qualifying achievement is not mentioned by any of the '49ers.

Also, in June of 1848, discharged members of the Mormon Battalion had brought a wagon with them over the trail to Salt Lake City. Still, no wagon train had been over it. Traveling such a trail with a few hardened men was one thing. Doing so with over a hundred wagons, including women and children, was another. But there seemed little choice. This late in the season it was the only way out.

So it was, at Hunt's $10 per wagon fee, the West's most famed wagon train set out from Provo, just south of Salt Lake

City, in early October of 1849. Just how many wagons there were varies according to accounts—from 84 to 125. Understandably the exact number is difficult to ascertain as late-comers joined, others dropped out and wagons broke down or were abandoned without factual recording. Reliably, one can accept the train as 100-plus wagons; three to five hundred men, women and children; plus some five hundred oxen, horses and mules.

Among those "lost" in the confusion and dust of the lengthening wagon train was Louis Nusbaumer and five companions: "Hadapp, Calverwell from Washington City, Fisch from Indiana, Isham from Michigan and a colored man named Smith from Missouri."*

Having started late, they traveled day and night to catch up, covering 208 miles in ten days before they joined the main body. And it was not an easy 20 mile a day average. The way was rocky, sandy, barren. Water was meager and when found was often so contaminated by dirt, debris and animals that the best one could say for it was that it was "wet", fit only for the desperate.

Doubts arose over Hunt's sureness of the trail. So it was that when a party of packers, men on horseback and mules, caught up with them with a rumor of a short-cut that could save 300 miles of such trail the emigrants listened. Especially since the leader of the packers, a "Captain Smith", purportedly had a map showing the short-cut, including sites for water without which survival was impossible.

Some doubted. Many believed. Most were tempted. As a result only seven of the wagons stayed with Hunt when they reached the turn off. Hunt, announcing that he had bargained to take them to Los Angeles over his route, bid farewell to the dissidents. "If all of you wish to go with Smith," he declared, "I will go also. But if even one wagon decides to go the original route I shall feel bound

*In other accounts, including Manly's, Calverwell is spelled "Culverwell", Fisch as "Fish" and Isham called "Graham". Since Nusbaumer knew these men more closely his spellings are used in this account.

by my promise to go with that lone wagon." And he added, "If you all decide to follow Smith I will go with you, even if the road leads to Hell."

It was to be a hell and of a reality which few realized.

"Immediately in front of us was a canyon, impassable for wagons . . .
we named this place Mt. Misery."

—William Manly

SHORT CUT TO HELL

On November 4, 1849, the wagon train separated near present day Cedar City, Utah. The seven wagons that elected to remain with Hunt watched the others, including Nusbaumer, depart on the "short-cut."

A few days later the short-cutters found themselves stranded in a seemingly impassable canyon-cleft area. The terrain had been deceptively easy; but now, with shocking suddenness they were brought to a halt. "Immediately in front of us was a canyon, impassable for wagons and down into this a trail descended. Men could go, horses and mules perhaps, but wagons could no longer follow."*

Searching parties went out early and returned late, with discouraging reports. Finally, on November 10, all of the wagons except 27 turned back to catch up with Hunt. Ironically, later that day a searching party reported that they had found a "pass"! And on November 11, the 27 wagons with some 95 men, women and children, continued along their "short-cut" to California.

It is uncertain from Nusbaumer's journal whether his party of six had started out from Salt Lake City afoot. But somewhere along the trail they did acquire a wagon. Perhaps one that had been abandoned, as a number were. Or one bought from some family who felt they could get by with one less wagon. Rather

---

Among one of the advance parties who descended the trail, which double-teamed wagons were to eventually attempt, was Henry W. Bigler. The site is identified by his still recognizable carvings into a cliff wall of the date and his initials. ("Sat. Nov. 3rd. Laid by until nearly noon for our animals to rest and eat grass. I cut the 3 first letters of my name on a Rock and the date".) Intriguingly, it was also Bigler who witnessed and recorded the discovery of gold at Coloma almost two years before.

"Sat., Nov. 3d. I cut the first 3 letters of my name on a rock and the date."

—Henry W. Bigler, Mt. Misery

strangely, he does not say. But then there were many other problems to occupy the mind and his small notebook-journals had too few pages on which to record everything.

At first, having escaped the rugged confines of "Mt. Misery", the traveling was comparatively pleasant. Morale soared. Surely the worst had been overcome. The spare, dry underbrush now gave way to greenery. The trees, while not large, provided a measure of shade and relief to eyes that had seen little more than sage, sand and sun for too many days. And now, in a higher elevation, the air was cooler. At night they built campfires. There was singing and fiddle playing. As one of the emigrants recalled:

> "Great fires, fed by greasewood, shot into lofty spires, imparting warmth and radiating cheer . . . Nat Ward played the old tunes on his violin and they who had music in their souls, though not perhaps in their throats, vexed the air with the old time songs . . ."

But their problems were not over. Not by far. Had they but known, they would have fought their way back up to "Mt. Misery" and fled back to the main trail as did the others. But clairvoyance is a gift given to few. If they were not already inclined to do so, they had learned along the trail to live each day and not look back. After all, they were in pursuit of a dream, and dreamers do not dwell unduly upon yesterday.

Gradually the wagon wheels rolled more and more slowly. They began descending into sandy valleys that seemed to have no streams, no forage. The bare, bleak ranges were north-south which, in their westward course, meant laboriously crossing steep ridges or going out of their way to find lower passes. And between were dry, salt-crusted playas of ancient lakes.

There seemed to be no end to the distances that extended far beyond which the eye could see. There was only dust, heat, thirst, despair. It appeared to be the most desolate land they had ever seen and would never hope to see again. On and on they went. There was little choice. It was too late to turn back. Besides, as an emigrant over another but somewhat similar trail voiced: "Turn

"We joined a company of six wagons which we met near one of the dry lakes."

—Nusbaumer, Papoose Dry Lake

25

back? What a chill the words send through one. Turn back? On a journey like that, in which every mile had been gained by most earnest labor, growing more and more intense until of late it had seemed that the certainty of *advance* with every step was all that made the next step possible . . ."

In the waning days of November they caught two Indians. By sign language, their only bond of communication, they learned that ". . . it was impossible to get through (on the course we were taking) as there was no water and the mountains were too steep to cross. They advised us to go farther south. They also showed us a spring at a time when our animals were just ready to give out for want of water. Unfortunately the men let the Indians go free when they could have assisted us as guides and we were left helpless without food and water amid the vast hilly plains of California."

They were not, of course, in "California". They were still in the wastelands of central Nevada. Fatefully, had they kept heading west they would have followed a route to be used years later to some of the early Nevada mining districts including Goldfield and Tonopah. However, as if to prove the susceptibility of men to will o' the wisp pursuits, they turned south. Not only because of the advice of the Indians, but as one of the emigrants was to write:

> "We saw, for the first time, a mirage . . . a sheet of water which all of us believed to be Owens Lake . . . they who gazed upon it had never known what wonderous power a mirage is capable of exerting . . . so strong was the impression of reality that disillusionment did not come until long after nightfall."

So it was that the phenomenon of a lake of water bordered by trees lured them on, only to prove an illusion created by heat waves arising from warm air radiating over still another dry lake bed. But, having gone fifty miles on this new course, they were now committed to continuing on. Although there were times when, in retrospect, they should have turned back they never did. They knew what they had been over. They did not know what lay ahead and could only feel it might be no worse and perhaps even better.

26

More than ever they began to string out, each segment struggling at its own pace, somewhat within sight of the others if only for swirls of dust in the distance, or simply following the tracks of those already lost to view. Those best able to do so drove desperately ahead. The stragglers, just as desperately, staggered into camps guided by their fires.

Numbed with the surprisingly bone-chilling cold of the desert on winter nights, parched by the dry heat of day, physically and mentally beat by deprivation and despair, they continued on through little more than force of habit.

So it was that, in early December, they entered what was to be the AEC's test site, familiarly known as "Frenchman Flat". For those to whom green grass and forests were almost second nature it was an incredible land of endless miles of nothing but rocks, and and stunted brush, of water holes that were a life—or death—apart, and of shimmering white dry lake beds.

It was at one of these, now known as Papoose Dry Lake, that the '49ers were to camp together for the last time. Despite later partial regroupings, the emigrants' unity now shattered like Humpty-Dumpty, never to be put together again.

On the morning of December 2, 1849, the Jayhawkers packed their meager belongings and left towards a dimly discerned pass to the west. Nusbaumer's little group decided to cast their lot and add their wagon to the six of the Bennett, Arcane and Wade families, as well as that of two brothers named Erhardt, traveling with two teen-age sons. Along with a few drivers to assist with the wagons the group numbered about 30, including eight children. The families might move slower but at least there was more unity of purpose than with the Jayhawkers who were increasingly splintering into dissident factions.

The families remained at Papoose Dry Lake for four more days, primarily waiting for their scout, William Lewis Manly, to return from his reconnoitering of the best route to take. Following the Jayhawker departures Manly notes:

27

'49er camp at Triple Tanks. 1849 inscription can be faintly seen between the center rock cavity and the bush to the left.

"Mr. Culverwell and Mr. Fish stayed with us making another wagon in our train. We talked the matter over carefully . . . to the south of us was a mountain that now had considerable snow upon its summit . . . (altho) it was quite off of our course . . . the prospects for reaching water were so much better in that way that we finally decided to go there rather than follow the Jayhawkers . . ."

Through Nye Canyon they headed for their sighting of 11,918' Mt. Charleston. Their goal was the snow, for snow meant water if simply by melting it over campfires. They did have food, however meager. Water was the urgent need, for men and animals. Both could survive longer without food and forage than without water.

Progress through the narrow canyon was slow. It was rocky, steadily ascending, twisting and filled with soft sand areas that bogged down the wagons again and again. For men and animals in prime condition it would have been task enough, but for those almost to the breaking point it was torturous.

Midway along the canyon they camped, huddled at the opening to a small ravine. Here, at what is known as Triple Tanks, they waited for two men who had left earlier to scout ahead. While waiting, one of the emigrants used his knife to carve "1849" in the sandstone cliff, marking their passage. Dulled by the cold and despair, they probably paid little heed to the Indian petroglyph carvings alongside. They could not read them, for the meanings have long been lost to man. But they might have deducted that this had been a well used campsite area for the Indians, who did so with water nearby. Ironically, later day miners and cowboys, perhaps out of curiosity, did follow this ravine to three natural "tanks" or basins of water a short distance away. But Fate is fickle and the emigrants remained at the entrance. Yet all was not lost, for Nusbaumer writes:

"We were sitting dejectedly around a fire planning to kill an ox and dry his meat and to carry our baggage on our backs when suddenly a 'hurrah!' filled us with new life and made me forget the pain in my hand. (I had accidently cut my thumb very badly.) We ran toward the spot from whence the shouts came and heard, to our greatest joy, that one of the scouts had found an Indian family about six miles from our camp, with good water and plenty of food. We also had learned from the Indians that Capt. Walker with some *Americans* had passed south of the 'farm.' The next day we hurried there to feed our cattle and to rest a few days and then, in God's name, to continue our trip to the Land of Gold."

The two scouts were William Manly and John Rogers. Manly, who was to later write his own classic account, and who had gotten the name "Walker" from the Indians, instinctively interpreted it as the Indian Chief "Walkara" of his earlier experiences back along the Green River approaching the Great Salt Lake. Walkara frequently crossed hundreds of miles of mountains and desert to raid California ranchos for horses. He may well have passed this way. And he was in truth an "American". Nusbaumer more correctly associated the information with famed mountain man Joe Walker, who had passed just south of here while following Fremont's 1844 Expedition on their return east. But strangely enough neither Manly, Nusbaumer, nor any of the others attached a logical conclusion to the information—that a nearby trail had been blazed or followed, be it by white man or Indian. Had they done so their tale would have known a different, happier ending.

The group remained at the "Indian farm" for nine days to recuperate man and beast at the best supply of water and grass they had seen for some time and might not see again. Then, on December 19, they hitched up the wagons and moved on—into Death Valley and history.

A noticeable change now takes place in Nusbaumer's entries. Up to this point much of his journal was written periodically as opportunity and inclination permitted. As if in a growing awareness there might not be another tomorrow, he now records the entries daily, and we share the events as they take place:

31

"December 19. Today we left the farm where we had been camping . . . and started for a spring which was said to be about seven miles from here. Tomorrow we intend marching fifteen miles. How varied are the ways of man. Fifteen years ago, about this same time in the year in my father's house, with its Christmas preparations—no sorrow, nothing but joy. Last year in Newark with my beloved wife. (Should I ever return to her I will never leave her again, not even for a day.) This year in the region of the California gold fields.

"Should we ever arrive on the other side of the Sierra Nevada it will be like the landing of a shipwrecked crowd for most of our clothing has become worn out in our nine months of travel and we may even throw away what we have left if it becomes necessary to carry our food and other baggage and march on foot. Let us keep up good hope!"

Poor Nusbaumer. He was not in the "region of the California gold fields." They were still hundreds of miles away. Even the miles to the spring they had hoped to find stretched on endlessly. The weather became increasingly warmer. Lips became parched and eyes burned from the swirling alkaline dust. Then, as they descended into a large low valley they found water! And not just a brackish seep, but—

"At the entrance of the valley on the right hand side we found a cave containing a spring with magnificent warm water . . . The cave is of a fairy like aspect. It seems we are on the road to a Happy Christmas!"

They had happily blundered into what is now called "Devil's Hole", a tiny, isolated island of Death Valley National Monument just east of the Nevada border.* A cave-pool that lies in a freakish

*The next known visitors to this cave-pool were those of the expedition of Nevada Governor Blasdel in 1886. While the cave is about 30' x 10', the depths of the water continuing beyond and beneath are seemingly bottomless. Several divers have been lost endeavoring to explore the depths, the "home" of unique blind minnows that have genetically lost their sight surviving in its dark recesses.

32

fault fissure at the base of some low volcanic cliffs. The water was palatable although warm. Indeed, Nusbaumer reports it as being about ninety degrees and providing a luxuriously enjoyable bath.

Morale was high when they left the next day, only to be shattered within hours. One of the oxen pulling Nusbaumer's wagon was about to give out. Without it they would have to backpack their supplies. And since far less could be carried the chances of survival would be correspondingly lessened. Since no outside observer from this point in time can quite recapture the touching pathos of the feelings experienced by Nusbaumer, let us turn back in time and watch over his shoulder as he writes:

"December 24. Twelve miles. Our prospects again look dismal. One of our oxen is about to die but we will not despair on the eve of the day when our Savior was born. We came about fifteen miles today through abominable alkali swamps and were compelled to camp without water and grass. In fact, we had to go back quite a distance to get water for our supper.

"December 25. Christmas day in the mountains of California,* written in camp just before leaving. This is a day of sorrow for us as the ox, before mentioned, is not able to go further and it is necessary for us to throw out a great deal of our goods in order to lighten the load . . . There is quite a difference between Christmas days in different states. In some of them you receive presents, in others you must throw things away. I hope my dear wife is having a happier Christmas day than I am. My God keep her in good health. Should I never return to her and should chance deliver this journal into her hands, she will glean from these pages that she was never far from my thoughts and that my heart will beat for her to the last."

* *Actually they were still in Nevada.*

"Dec. 23 . . . we found a cave containing a spring with magnificent warm water in which Hadapp and I took a refreshing bath."

—Nusbaumer, Devil's Hole, Nevada.

35

29ᵗ July 1849.
Chimney Rock
Rattelsnake, Sioux
30ᵗ d. Sioux town 31ᵗ J
Aug. Algind Sioux Sut
Major McDaule
3ᵗ Fort Laramie
17 Aug August Bear

A page from Nusbaumer's journal, showing his sketch of Chimney Rock along the overland trail.

36

INTO THE VALLEY OF DEATH

The small group of wagons and families threading their way into Death Valley had begun to straggle apart. Some, in better condition, moved on ahead, leaving the others to catch up when— and if—they could. One of these was the Brier family. No less poignant than Nusbaumer's thoughts of Christmas were Julia Brier's recollection:

> "We reached the top of the divide between Death and Ash valleys and oh, what a desolate country we looked down into. The next morning we started down. The men said they could see what looked like springs out in the valley. Mr. Brier was always ahead to explore and find water so I was left with our three boys to help bring up the cattle . . . Poor little Kirk gave out and I carried him on my back, barely seeing where I was going, until he would say, 'Mother, I can walk now.' Poor little fellow. He would stumble on a little way over the salty marsh and sink down crying 'I can't go on any farther.' Then I would carry him again and soothe him as best I could . . .
>
> "Night came and we lost all track of those ahead. I would get down on my knees and look in the starlight for the ox tracks and then we would stumble on. There was not a sound and I didn't know whether we would ever reach camp or not. About midnight we came around a big rock and there was my husband at a small fire. 'Is this camp?' I asked. 'No, it's six miles farther,' he said. I was ready to drop and Kirk was almost unconscious, moaning for a drink. Mr. Brier took him on his back and hastened to camp to save his little life. It was 3 o'clock Christmas morning when we reached the spring—a Christmas none could ever forget."

Despite the darkness and despair, contact lost between them, the various parties struggled on, with Nusbaumer's group trailing far behind. As feared, they had to abandon their wagon and trudge

37

on afoot. And, like the others, were channeled into the canyon that seemingly offered the only route westward through the mountains. But at least, although they knew it not and possibly were beyond caring, they were at long last "in the mountains of California."

But it was not the lush greenery, the meadowlands saddle high in grass, the cooling ocean breezes they had pictured California to be. There were no great oaks, no picturesque missions, no welcoming greetings in either strange or familiar tongues, no sleek cattle or grazing sheep, no fields of grain—and no mines of gold. There was only stark desolation. Bare, bleak mountains where even scrub brush struggled to survive. Sun-scorched rocks and sand without end. And in the gap before them they saw the awesome expanse of Death Valley.

They had seen similar valleys since leaving "Mt. Misery." But those had been smaller, less formidable and relatively easier to traverse. That which lay before them staggered the imagination and crushed the spirit. They had been through so much. Surely now they could not be expected to do more than they had ever done before. They had been traveling since spring and it was now the end of December. They should have been filling their pockets with gold months before, but there was only sand, salt, the heat of the sun by day and biting cold at night.

But almost to the very edge of the valley they came upon a spring, the finest in the entire area. Indeed, several springs that joined to form a small but flowing stream. Here, at Travertine Springs, close to today's Furnace Creek Inn, Nusbaumer's little group caught up with the other '49ers including Manly's contingent of families.

Various groupings of the splintered Jayhawkers had gone north up the valley to where they thought they could see a pass over the large mountain range on the other side. "It seemed," said Manly, "there were many men from the various parties scattered all around the country, each one seeking out the path which seemed to suit best his tender feet or present fancy, steering west as well as mountains and canyons would permit; some farther north, some farther south, and generally demoralized, each thinking that

38

as a last resort he would be able to save his own life . . . Both men and oxen were shod with moccasins made of rawhide to protect the feet against sharp rocks. They could see no trail, but merely picked out the best way to go . . . They killed some of their oxen and took the wood of their wagons and kindled fires to dry and smoke the flesh so it would be light and easy to carry with them. They scattered all surplus baggage around the ground, carefully storing and saving the bit of bread that yet remained and dividing it equally among the party. They also divided the tea, coffee, rice and some such things, and each one agreed that he could not ask aught of his neighbor more."

Watching the Jayhawkers leave to the north the families spent hours debating whether to follow. Not without misgivings they decided to go south where the mountains did seem to lower. The English family of the Wades — with mother, father, four children and at least one assistant driver, an Alsatian named Schaub—trailed at the rear as was their custom.

But Nusbaumer's sextet, now only a trio, remained behind. Fisch and Isham had left to follow the Jayhawkers, Both, older men, were to perish not long after. According to Edward Coker the "colored man named Smith" had evidently left far back at Papoose Dry Lake, joining one of the Jayhawker groups at that point.

Calverwell was too ill to go on. Nusbaumer and Hadapp elected to stay with him until he had recuperated sufficiently so they could go on together. What the feelings might have been as they watched the others leave is not known, only suspected. But to abandon poor "Captain" Calverwell, aged and ailing, was unthinkable.

The 29th, 30th and 31st of December were wiled away drying ox meat and making other preparations. Touchingly, Nusbaumer's entry for January 1st (1850) begins with, "Happy New Year! The first of January, 1850!" It must have been a quiet celebration. Yet, incredibly their faith was not unrewarded for—

Den 25t. December 1849
Californiens. —

Dieser Zug war ein allzu
abenteuerliche [illegible] nicht mehr ein
[illegible] waren alle auf-
um den Bergen so weit zu [illegible]
[illegible] kann. Das [illegible]
[illegible]
[illegible] für 1 [illegible] etc. &
[illegible] Büchlein, 3 [illegible]
[illegible] & meinen Mantel
[illegible] ist krank & hatte auch
[illegible] zu Hause [illegible]
zu erreichen [illegible]
[illegible] zu behalten & oder
unseren Kräften [illegible]
mittel [illegible]
nicht [illegible] & wir hatten
Ziel doch noch zu erreichen. Als
[illegible] in d. Händen Gottes
mein Gedanken, x) ein [illegible]
[illegible]!) Ich wünsche mein
Weihnachtsfest zu feiern als auch
& wäre [illegible] zu derselben zu[illegible]
stellte ihr mein Tagebuch ein
[illegible], dass sie ein
[illegible] bis zum letzten Augenblick

The entry for Christmas Day, 1849, as written by Nusbaumer approaching Furnace Creek and Death Valley.

"December 25, 1849. Christmas day in the mountains of California, written in camp just before leaving.

This is a day of sorrow for us as the ox, before mentioned, is not able to go further and it is necessary for us to throw out a great deal of our goods in order to lighten the load so one yoke of oxen can pull it. Here I had to leave behind five good linen shirts, boots, handkerchiefs, one coat, friend Adolph's hat, stockings and buffalo hide, etc., and only took three shirts, my black cashmere coat, one pair stockings, one pair of boots, one pair of shoes, one buffalo hide and my cloak and so did the rest. Friend Hadapp who also had to sacrifice his best things is sick. If we succeed in reaching the company ahead of us we intend to load one ox with food and to wander on if our strength, which is very much broken down by poor nourishment, permits us. Courage has not failed us yet and we hope with God's help to reach our destination.

There is quite a difference between Christmas days in different states. In some of them you receive presents, in others you must throw things away. I hope my dear wife is having a happier Christmas day than I am. May God keep her in good health. Should I never return to her and should chance deliver this journal into her hands, she will glean from these pages that she was never far from my thoughts and that my heart will beat for her to the last."

Translation of Nusbaumer's Christmas Day entry.

42

"Two Alsatians took pity on our condition and provided us with boiled beans. Thus we began the New Year quite cheerfully, while two or three days ago we were almost in despair. We exchanged a pistol for beans and coffee and are now living in comparative affluence. Today (on the 2nd of January) we had excellent soup. We boiled ox feet and snout with beans for a whole night and as a result we had a fine mulligan this morning which revived us . . . Blessed New Year dear wife and perhaps child."*

Just who the two good Samaritans were is lost to history. Of four Alsatians only two are known by name: Schaub, the Wade's driver, and an Anton Schlogel who was to make a more pronounced appearance later.

On the 7th of January the remaining three members of Nusbaumer's group moved out and "traveled for about eight miles without water and not anticipating that we would find any. As viewed from the top of the mountain the whole valley seemed to be filled with it but on approaching the same it proved to be clear salt water. We even had to march through salt puddles and dry salt."

Like those ahead they had to cross over the west side of the great saline sink, perhaps following their trail.

"On the 8th," Nushbaumer continues, "it was very much the same. Hadapp and I had such an overpowering thirst we even tried to drink the salt water. It was here I tried to exchange my coat and two shirts for a drink of water. We had overtaken two wagons carrying ample water but we failed to obtain any. The man who refused to give us water was forced to abandon an ox on account of sickness. We shot him and caught his blood in a vessel and drank it down, only regretting that there was not more of it to quench our thirst. This only made us more thirsty. We continued on our way until one o'clock at night when we lay down under a bush and tried to forget our miserable condition by sleeping."

*This would have been his son Albert, born after his father's departure for California.

43

"As viewed from the top of the mountains the whole valley seemed to be filled with water, but it proved to be salt."

—Nusbaumer, Death Valley

McLean Spring, Death Valley, where the Jayhawkers burned their
wagons and set out on foot.

Reassuringly, Nusbaumer later clarifies that it was the abandoned ox they shot and not the man!

On the 13th day they found a companion in misery:

". . . an Alsatian by the name of Anton Schlogel . . . He had three yoke of oxen but after traveling for several miles one of his oxen took sick and was unable to go further. We therefore decided to join our lots and promised never to desert one another but to help each other and to divide our provisions. We killed the ox, took his tongue and heart and liver and followed after the company ahead when suddenly we saw them returning and also turned back."

What happened was that the Bennetts, Arcanes and Wades, who had gone ahead, had reached the opening to a canyon that seemed to promise passage through the Panamint mountains. Laboriously they had inched their wagons up the alluvial slopes— to a deadend. They now had to turn back down into the valley again. Here, on the 14th of January, 1850, they halted at a small seep of brackish water. It was, according to Manly:

". . . a mound about four feet high and in the top of this a little well that held about a pailfull of water that was quite strong of sulphur. When stirred it would look quite black. About the mouth of the well was 'wire grass' that seemed to prevent its caving in. It seems the drifting sand had slowly built this little mound about the well of water in a curious way. We spent the night here and kept a man at the well all night to keep the water dipped out as fast as it flowed in order to get enough for ourselves and cattle . . ."

They knew not where they were, or how to escape from the seemingly inevitable fate of starvation and thirst. There were endless discussions about the campfire, whether to go this way or that, whether to strike out on foot or endeavor to find another route for the wagons.

That night a meeting was held and Bennett proposed:

48

". . . we select two of our youngest, strongest men . . . and ask them to try to seek a settlement and food and we will go back to the good spring we have just left and wait for their return. It will surely not take them more than ten days . . ."

Nusbaumer's foursome had apparently started to follow the wagons up the slope, then spotted them returning from the abortive attempt. They were together at the brackish spring meeting for when Manly left he noted, "We received all sorts of advice. Captain Culverwell was an old seafaring man and was going to tell us how to find our way back . . ." But rather than stay at this poor supply of water, those remaining backtracked up the valley several miles to a better spring that they had found earlier, which was to be their historic "Long Camp".

Here they settled down for what they hoped would be the agreed upon ten days for Manly and Rogers to return. But the days went by slowly. There were increasing doubts as to whether the two could get through. What if the would-be rescuers were attacked by Indians? Or had fallen along the perilous slopes? Or had perished of hunger and lack of water? They might not know until too late to wait much longer. Little did they know that it was to take 26 days for Manly. and Rogers to travel some 250 miles to Los Angeles and another 250 miles to return.

The Wades were among those who decided not to wait. After a few days of wrestling with their conscience, and understandably aware of the dependency of their four small children, the Wades left camp along with Schaub their Alsatian wagon driver. But instead of again trying to penetrate the mountains to the west the Wades drove southerly. Although there was not even a sign of greenery to indicate water, at least the mountains were lower and perhaps they could find a crossing.

Nusbaumer, Calverwell, Hadapp and Schlogel were wracked with indecision. They had learned that there was safety in numbers. Not only against Indians but in the sharing of supplies, the aid and comfort one could extend to another. But on the eleventh day they too gave up hope and started south.

A rare unpublished picture of '49er William Lewis Manly

Harry and Mary Wade, whose four children were 5 to 14 years old
at the time of their Death Valley experiences. It was the Wade's trail
south from the "Long Camp" that Nusbaumer's small group followed.
The Wade's wagon was the only one brought out of Death Valley by
the '49ers.

53

The ten days they had spent in the "Long Camp" were not very recuperative. Nusbaumer noticed a swelling in his legs and hands. Hadapp was having the same trouble. Apparently both were becoming victims of scurvy. Nonetheless they started out—only to be forced back.

"On the fourth day," Nusbaumer writes, "we turned back because we were not able to get through. My feet were swollen to such an extent that I could not put on my socks and had to cut open my shoes to the toes and even then it was only with the greatest difficulty that I was able to walk. My whole body from my chest down was swollen to abnormal proportions. The cause of the disease is incomprehensible to me. Can it be the water, our mode of living, or the air? It is doubtful whether I shall survive or succumb."

Even more slowly than they had sought to escape they struggled back toward camp. But before reaching it, and in a little side canyon, they found a small spring. And, about the same time met Wade and Schaub who informed them that they had found a trail westerly. Was Wade right? Was it a trail by which they could continue? There had been so many false hopes. Wade, especially with a wagon, might find this to be another abortive effort. Perhaps it would be best to wait and see. Besides, they were in no condition to follow Wade just then. So it was they returned to the "Long Camp" where the others were huddled in the meager shelter of the mesquite trees that offered at least token shade from the sun and branches to fuel the campfires at night.

As a measure of the physical and mental distress that must have prevailed we may reflect that on January 19, four days after Nusbaumer watched Manly and Rogers disappear into the mountains, he failed to note that he had attained his 31st birthday in the Valley of Death.

Indeed, the days and dates had blended and blurred one into another. But while they rested as best they could for still another escape effort, Nusbaumer continued his journal, writing by the light of flickering fires in a fearful land in which they were the first known white men. Fortunately his dedication in doing so provides the only known datings for what happened at the time.

54

THE ESCAPE

Nusbaumer's entry for February 1 records ". . . we are await-ing a signal from one of the scouts who went ahead to see if the trail which Wade proposed taking was practicable and if water and grass could be found. Should this be the case the following day will find us on the way. Schlogel and I have sworn friendship forever and should I make my fortune at the diggings I am deter-mined to return with him to Quincy (Illinois), there to buy a farm or start a business of some kind and take my whole family there in order to provide them with a life of contentment."

They waited almost a week longer. And on February 7 six others joined Nusbaumer, Hadapp, Calverwell and Schlogel in still another and possibly final effort to escape from the deadly valley that had imprisoned them for over six weeks.

Of the six, four were Ehrhardts—father, brother and two young sons—and the others the two unnamed Alsatians. It is one of life's injustices that their names and fates are lost among the blank pages of history.

Once again Nusbaumer's journal is fragmented by missing pages. And not surprisingly. His "journal" was actually two small pocket notebooks, one of about 68 pages, the other about 50. Cheaply stitched with string the pages were all too easily loosened and lost. The wonder is that they survived as well as they did. Worn, sweat-stained, dog-eared, each precious page was filled with his tightly written entries. Perhaps the missing pages slipped out and were lost in the wind, or used to light a badly needed fire. Or in the over a hundred years for the journal to come to light others may have carelessly lost the loose pages. Quien sabe?

At least the fragmented portions at this period can be pieced in with the recollections of others. So it is that we can number the original "Long Camp" parties as having been 19 adults and 8 children, 27 in all. Of these 8 were to eventually escape with Man-ly and Rogers. 7 were to leave with Wade, including his family of six plus Schaub. The other ten were Nusbaumer's newly formed group who began a forced march to catch up with the Wades.

Whether they did is uncertain. Nusbaumer does not note it and surely he would have. In his fragmented pages at this point we can discern only that one day, almost perishing of thirst, his group fanned out to search for water. As they rendezvoused back at camp Nusbaumer was shocked to discover Calverwell had not returned, nor could they find him. Apparently, out of sight of each other while looking for water, Calverwell had collapsed and was unable to signal for help. Facing the desperate realities of survival, the others had little choice than to continue on. In a country where weeks of searching could be unrewarding, the loss of one man had to be weighed against the loss of all.

But Calverwell may well have chanced upon the Wades. In 1894 a family friend of the Wades wrote an article for the *San Jose Pioneer* newspaper, in which she tells:

> "One evening in one of their (Wades') dry camps they were overtaken by a Mr. Colwell (Calverwell) who was almost famished. 'Oh' he said, 'if I could only get at my mother's swill barrel what a feast I would have tonight.' As they could not help him he went on but failing to find water perished alone on the sands."

One can only wonder, if indeed this report is true, how little a share of food and water it would have taken to save the life of a man barely able to crawl into the Wade camp. And to muse over the irony that the Wades' wagon was the only one to survive the Death Valley trek!

Yet such decisions were not easily made. If there was scarcely sufficient provisions for a family would it still be so if shared with even just one more? Looking at the gaunt faces and weakened bodies, listening to the cries of the young, may well have hardened hearts otherwise more compassionate.

Tragically, the very next day, as Manly and Rogers returned to Death Valley, they found the body of "Captain" Calverwell.

"He did not look much like a dead man." Manly notes, "He lay upon his back with arms extended wide and his little canteen, made of two powder flasks, lying at his side. This looked indeed as if some our saddest forebodings were coming true. How many more bodies should we find? Or should we find the camp deserted, with never a trace of the former occupants?"

Poor Calverwell. True, he was an elderly man to whom the rigors of the overland journey were more of a strain than for the others. True, too, he had been ill and ailing; the reason for his having been left behind once before at Fort Kearney by his original company and of which his son was a member. And then, Fate's unkind finale, to have him die one day before Manly and Rogers were to find him! Had they arrived earlier they might have saved him. Perhaps not. One will never know.

In the meantime, Nusbaumer's party struggled on. One week, two weeks passed. Although they worked their way toward higher elevations there seemed no end to the sandy valleys, the dry lake beds, the despairing views of sparse, stunted brush and, if they were lucky, small seeps of brackish water.

On the 21st of February, two weeks after Calverwell's disappearance, Nusbaumer writes:

> "On the 21st we started late . . . and made only fifteen miles. It was well for us three—Hadapp, Schlogel and myself—that we joined these people for had we been alone we never would have been able to carry our provisions and water. Hadapp and I intend paying them thirty dollars, should we have the good luck, to Jake Ehrhardt, from Iowa, that he has been so kind and generous to us and I will try to reward him in every way possible."

Deductively, the four Ehrhardts had clung to their wagon. Certainly Nusbaumer's gratitude that without the others they would never have been able to transport his trio's provisions provides strong inference of a wagon—unless one can far-fetchedly picture the supplies being backpacked by men also nearing the end

The desolate view across Death Valley from Bennetts Well where the "Long Camp" waited a month for rescue.

An old view of Bennetts Well, when there was water, a windmill and road sign.

of their strength and burdened by their own provisions. The fate of this wagon will in all likelihood never be known. Someday, perhaps, bits and pieces may yet be found bleaching in the sun, although more likely they were long ago used for fuel by early miners or borax men, or hopelessly intermixed with their own discards. Indicatively, Schlogel's wagon had been abandoned at the "Long Camp".

On February 22 they reached, miracle of miracles, the Mojave River! It was a sight the likes of which they had not seen since leaving the area of the Great Salt Lake almost four months back. As important as this was, their cup of joy brimmed over with the signs of horses' hoof prints! It was not only a sign of man, but pointed out a trail to follow. Soberly Nusbaumer comments:

> "It seemed that God, who has so far protected us, will guide us soon to our destination. I believe that most of us have changed, not only in body but in mind; no longer wishing for wealth, but content to lead a quiet life with our families and to return home with a smaller sum than we anticipated when starting out."

Then he adds, "HURRAH FOR CALIFORNIA!" Just three words, large and boldly written, and in English as if to emphasize that his Americanization had passed the crucible's test.

It lessens not the joy to observe they had actually been "Californians" since December 24th when they entered Death Valley. Or to wryly muse that the loss of desire for wealth was to last only a few months, until Nusbaumer joined the gold rush along the Merced River. And that he never did return to Quincy with Schlogel.

On the first of March, just twenty days short of a year since he left his wife, Nusbaumer "feasted" at a Spanish ranch on ". . . beef and corn, the best meal I have ever tasted. We ate so heartily that it almost takes our breath away."

Undoubtedly he also learned to his dismay that Hunt, who continued with the wagons that did not take the "short cut", had arrived at this Spanish ranch two months before.

Continuing to Los Angeles, two days later, Nusbaumer found work as a teamster at two dollars and a half a day and board. Here he ends his journal on a nostalgically sad note:

> "In Pueblo de Los Angeles received the news that Fisch and Isham had succumbed of hunger. Smith was killed by Pi Utes.* Of the six of us, Hadapp and myself are all that is left."

*When, where and even if Smith perished on the trek is uncertain. The report may simply have been hearsay, passed from one group to another. The news of Isham and Fisch, the two who had left Nusbaumer back at Travertine Springs on the 28th day of December 1849 had been brought to Los Angeles by the Jayhawkers who arrived early in February.

OF ISHAM, FISCH, SMITH
—AND THE JAYHAWKERS

Unfortunately there is no single chronicler of the Jayhawker travels and travail. That which is known of their wanderings, their separations and rejoinings, can only be pieced together from a number of recollections.

In leaving the camp where they burned their wagons, at what is now mapped as McLean Spring, near the junction of the Beatty-Stovepipe Wells-Furnace Creek roads, the Jayhawkers first headed up steep slopes toward a high crevice of snow. Water was the crying need. Such snows offered the promise of rivulets from the warming sun, possibly springs, or at least water from the patient melting of snow in kettles over the campfires.

At this "snow camp" the historic group was also to give birth to another of Death Valley's legends. That of the famous "Lost Gunsight Lode" for which men have searched for over a hundred years. As one of the Jayhawkers was to recall:

> "There were in camp some men from Georgia who were old silver miners. They told us that there was an immense wealth of silver in sight where we camped. One of them showed me a chunk of black rock he held in his hands and told me it was half silver and if we only had provisions and water and knew where we were, there was all the wealth in sight we could ask."

This may have been viewed skeptically by some or, considering their condition, with an understandable lack of enthusiasm. One of the men, having lost the sight of his rifle, crudely fashioned a new one out of this blackish rock. Eventually, when he reached Los Angeles and took his rifle to a gunsmith for a new sight he was informed that his makeshift gunsight was indeed almost pure silver!

What is more, while at this camp some of the men lightened their load by burying several thousand dollars in gold coins, wrapped in a blanket, under a greasewood bush which was to mark the spot should they ever be able to return. Several years later some

65

of them did return, but a cloudburst had obliterated all signs. Even the black, silver-rich rock which they had seen so abundantly on the surface had disappeared, perhaps buried under an avalanche of rain-loosened mud from the higher slopes.

Then, too, there is the story of John Goler's gold.

Goler and another German were inseparable companions. They spoke little or no English, and perhaps because of this language barrier did not mix with the other Jayhawkers. Known simply as "the two Dutchmen" by the others they traveled, camped and cooked together, invariably apart from their fellow travelers. One day, shortly after the wagons were burned and left behind, these two were out hunting for water. As one sat down to rest the other called out from nearby—"See what I have found!" The other asked if it was water. "No, it is gold!" Quickly came the reply, "I want no gold now. I want water and bread, which gold will not buy in this place. I would not pick it up here. Let us go and see if we can find water or we will soon die."

So the two moved on, like those that found the "Gunsight" silver, leaving a possible fortune. Although gold and silver were what they had come to the West to find, it was not worth the weight to carry when water was so much more precious.

After cresting the Panamint Range the Jayhawkers descended into yet another valley—almost, but not quite, the twin of Death Valley. And beyond were more mountains, ridge upon ridge. It was a sight to dismay even the strongest spirit and to disintegrate such semblance of unity they had managed to maintain.

As they reached the floor of this valley, the Panamint Valley, small groupings were fanning out towards unseen but hoped-for passes in the almost impassable barrier of the Argus Range.

Some of the slower travelers, including the Brier family, lingered behind at a small spring near Ballarat. There were seven in the Brier group, but after crossing the valley they met six others who had failed to find a way up and through the mountains. Among these were Fisch and Isham, the two who had left Nusbaumer, Hadapp and Calverwell at Travertine Springs two weeks before.

66

Striking out for what appeared to be the most promising canyon they soon found the way blocked by great rock falls. On each side there were "great walls rising up—oh, as high as we could see almost!" There seemed to be no way out of this deep and silent sepulcher. They turned back to where a slope to the north offered a foothold. It was a steep climb; and for one the exertion was fatal:

> "Father Fisch took hold of the tail of his ox and was helped out of the dismal canyon. He held onto the tail three or four hundred yards when he reeled and fell to rise no more. The boys were so excited they forgot to leave him his blankets and sent back for him the next day but he was dead."

Although Mrs. Brier softens the account by adding she had made coffee for Fisch, one winces that any of them could be so "excited" as to desert a companion to die alone in the darkness of a lonely and forbidding land—a fate that might well be theirs later on.

On and on they struggled. Cresting the ridge they looked down into still another valley. Nestled in its sandy setting was a small shallow lake. Alas, its shallow waters proved bitterly unpalatable. Startlingly, around it were small campfires of the Jayhawkers who had left the Briers days before. Coincidentally, in the angling courses, endeavoring to follow terrain of least resistance, the trails had crossed.

Water! Surely there had to be water! But where? As they spread out to search Isham fell behind. The search went on until finally one man wandered into a small canyon. According to his account he looked up to see five Indians with bows drawn, ready to shoot him. He managed, by signs, to tell them that he was hunting water. The Indians took hold of his tattered shirt as if they wanted it. He parted with it. In turn they threw a fine Indian blanket over his bare shoulders and pointed to water. He could hear it but not see it at first, hidden as it was by bushes. Happily he hurried back to the others with the news! Appropriately they christened it "Providence Spring."

67

Somewhat at variance with this version is that of Mrs. Brier:

"We were without a drop of water for 48 hours when at last we came upon two Germans of the company who had gone ahead. They were cooking at a tiny fire. 'Any water?' asked my husband. 'There's vasser,' one said, pointing to a muddy puddle . . . It was awful stuff but it saved our lives. A little later we came to a beautiful cold spring. Oh, how good it was. I always believed Providence placed it there to save us for it was such an unlikely spot."

In any event, some hurried back along the trail with water for those who had not yet arrived. They found that Isham had crawled for four miles on his hands and knees. He was still alive, but his mouth, tongue and throat were so swollen and parched that he could no longer swallow. While they bathed his hands and body he died.

But the renewed spirits did not end the dissension. Again the party divided. One segment went north, leaving in their wake a tantalizing clue to the least known member of the original Nusbaumer sextet—the "colored man named Smith". Edward Coker, leader of this party, was to tell that one of their party "was a colored man who joined us at the camp where we left the families (i.e., Papoose Dry Lake, back in Nevada), he being the only remaining member of a small party . . . made up of a Mr. Culverwell, a man named Fish and another man whose name I never knew." Unfortunately he does not mention Smith again, nor any incident that might indicate his demise by Indians as Nusbaumer was to hear.

The details of the rest of the Jayhawker travels are best left to other sources, and are of primary interest to historians. It is sufficient to note that except for one death and the disappearance of an unnamed Frenchman who wandered away and turned up again years later, all of the others reached the sanctuary of the San Fernando Valley, near Los Angeles, by the end of the first week in February, 1850, three weeks before Nusbaumer arrived.

OF CALVERWELL, FISCH, ISHAM—AND MANLY

Only one group was to reach the Los Angeles area after Nusbaumer. The Bennetts and Arcanes, with Manly and Rogers as their guides and rescuers.

After leaving their party at what became the "Long Camp", Manly and Rogers ascended the steep slopes of the Panamint Range that had barred the earlier attempt to escape with wagons. They had been given ten days to find help and return. Little did they know, and best that they did not at the time, it was to take them 26 days!

By the time they had finished their preparations and bid their farewells it was probably close to mid-day when they left. That night was spent high up on the slopes. They ascended to a pass the next morning, and in tribute to a man who could still see beauty amid such desolation it is fitting to quote Manly's recollection:

> "From this pass was the grandest sight we ever beheld. Looking east we could see the country we had been crawling over since early November . . . To the north was the biggest mountain we ever saw—peaks on peaks towering far above our heads . . . Southward was a nearly level plain and to the west I thought I could dimly see a range of mountains that held a little snow upon their summits, but on the range to the south there was none. It seemed to me the dim snowy mountains must be as far as two hundred miles away but of course I could not judge accurately."

In the clarity of the desert air distances were deceptive. And like modern moon-walking there were no landmarks, nothing to gauge by. Actually the dimly discerned snowy mountains were the Sierra Nevada, about 70 miles away. But this was as the crow flies. Manly and Rogers had to go this way then that, seeking a traversible way down the slopes and canyons into Panamint Valley which the Jayhawkers had entered via a more northerly route, and who had "found an Indian trail over a very steep pass to the west" out of Panamint Valley.

Crossing the valley at dusk they encountered the trail of the Jayhawkers. Following it the next morning they came to the body of Fisch lying in the sun. At the brackish water lake from which the Jayhawkers and Briers were forced to search for, and fortunately find, their "Providence Spring" about six miles away, the two scouts either lost the trail in the maze of footprints in all directions, or decided to follow their own instincts. Whatever the reason, the two canted southwesterly. There was simply no way of knowing of the providential spring. The Jayhawkers had left no messages for they little knew that any would follow.

At the base of the Sierra, across Indian Wells Valley, Manly and Rogers caught up with a group of the Jayhawkers. The camp-fires and conversations continued long and late that night as each filled the other in on all that had happened since they parted in Death Valley. Manly told how the "Long Camp" families had tried to take their wagons across the mountains and had to turn back to the spring where they were awaiting his and Rogers' return. In turn the Jayhawkers reported the deaths of Fisch and Isham, and told about the "Providence Spring" which Manly and Rogers had missed.

Manly and Rogers pushed on. On the 11th day of their rescue mission they saw a tree that had been *cut* down, with a nearby excavation about 4 feet square. This was the first indication of white men they had seen, and the hole was an apparent attempt at mining. Little did they know they were near the scene of California's first "gold rush", in 1842, close to the San Fernando Mission.

Then there was a sight best told in Manly's own words to appreciate the impact of what they now gazed upon compared to what they had looked at for so long:

> "Before us now was a spur from the hills . . . and a beautiful meadow of a thousand acres . . . and a herd of cattle numbering many hundreds if not thousands. Tears of joy ran down our faces."

70

They killed one of the steers and spent the night roasting and drying the meat, one sleeping while the other kept the fire. Some of the hide was used to make crude moccasins for their almost bare and bleeding feet.

The next day they saw a man and woman in the distance. They did not hail them, which might seem strange except for Manly's comment that they were a little afraid to meet anyone while they were wearing fresh rawhide on their feet. Hesitating to acknowledge killing one of the cattle without asking, unsure whether these were the owners and their reaction, Manly and Rogers continued on. A few hours later several men on horseback came galloping up. One was a white man who directed them to a small ranch a few miles away. Here they were given food, water, shelter and horses. Although the Spanish residents of the ranch could speak no English, sign language and the obvious condition of the two men bridged any language barrier.

Several days later, after progressing to the Mission, they returned to the ranch and were shown a small mill and how to grind flour for themselves. They were also given a sack of small yellow beans, a sack of wheat, a quantity of good fried meat and shown how to pack the horses properly.

> "I took what money we had and put it on a block, making signs for them to take what the things were worth. They took thirty dollars, and we were quite surprised to get two horses, the provisions, packsaddles, knapsacks and rawhide ropes so cheaply."

Touchingly, the woman of the ranch gave them four oranges, one for each child that Manly indicated that they had left behind. But curiously Manly had left eight children in camp. When he had left he had noted the Wades and could not have known of their subsequent departure. Was it a slip of memory or a deliberate slighting? Certainly one cannot help but toy with the picture of the four Wade youngsters seeing or hearing of the oranges for the others. And while it may have turned out to be half an orange for eight children, hopefully the discrepancy is simply one of re-

71

calling the count in retrospect, corrected by what he later knew. Lending credence to the latter, in his original account he writes of telling the woman at the ranch that they had left three women in the desert. In his "Vermont to California" version he says two. Mindful of the accuracy of his memory on so many things so many years later he can well be forgiven for these minor flaws.

By this time fifteen days had passed. Retracing their steps would likely take almost as long. They had been allotted ten. It was doubtful that the families could survive for twenty five to thirty days. It could mean going back, some 250 miles, in vain. And then retracing the 250 miles again. And what if the families had given up hope and moved on? To search for them in that vast desert wasteland would be hopeless.

Wracked by doubts and conscience, their thoughts that "If no women and children were out there we would not go back" are understandable. True, some of the men left behind had been companions since they started west in April, but—

Well, such reflections matter not. Whatever their doubts, however qualified their motives, Manly and Rogers did go back, facing days and weeks of difficult trail, deprivation and danger, not knowing what they would find back at the "Long Camp".

Truly no greater love hath any man than to be willing to lay down his life for another.

At least there was one consolation to the return trip. They knew from their earlier experience where there was water and grass for the animals. They did not have to waste time searching, nor were tormented by wondering what sources, if any, lay ahead. And thanks for the information gained from the Jayhawkers they now knew about Providence Spring.

From that spring they turned southwards towards the little valley with the alkaline lake on February 5, their 22nd day.

> "Near the eastern edge," Manly recalls, "we turned aside to visit the grave of Mr. Isham, which the Jayhawkers had told us of. Our next camp was on the summit of the range just before us and we passed the dead body of

72

Mr. Fisch, which we had seen before. We continued to a level spot large enough to sleep. The whole range is a black, rocky piece of earth. We tied our horses to rock and there stayed the night."

On the 26th day, February 9, they worked their way down into Death Valley and at its edge found the body of Captain Calverwell.

Continuing on, with heavy hearts, about noon Manly and Rogers came in sight of the wagon camp, still miles away. There was no sign of life. Nothing stirred. As they approached they could see four wagons and wondered, "Surely we left seven."

Unable to wait, they impulsively fired a shot. And as if by magic they saw a man come out from under a wagon and heard him shout, "The boys have come! The boys have come!"

One can fill in with his own instinctive understanding the conversations as Manly and Rogers reunited with the families. And to picture the preparations that were hastily made to leave.

On February 12th, 1850, the group moved out. They did not know what had happened to the Wades, Nusbaumer and many of the others with whom they had started out from Mt. Misery. They could not look back—except as they were leaving. From a ridge overlooking the great valley they turned momentarily to see that which they had overcome and emotionally cried out its historic naming—"Goodbye, Death Valley!"

In leaving, however otherwise they lightened their load, a shovel was taken along "so we might bury the body of Captain Culverwell." The Bennetts and Arcanes had told that Culverwell was among the last groups to leave. And Manly adds, "I afterwards learned that he could not keep up with them and turned to go back to the wagons again, and perished, stretched out upon the sand as we saw him, dying all alone, with no one to transmit his last words to family or friends. Not a morsel to eat, and the little canteen by his side empty. A sad and lonely death indeed."

They passed Fisch's body. Although at no time were they to note burying it, it is most likely they did at least cover it with sand

73

and rocks as protection against wild animals. And they passed, thoughtfully, the grave of Mr. Isham.

From Providence Spring to the camp where Manly and Rogers met the Jayhawkers, and on along the trail to the south, the details are of import more for historians delving deeply into the various accounts.

It is not that the trail was now easy. Far from it. It was a difficult trail. The women and children especially had to be spurred on with descriptions of water, grass, trees and cattle that had been found at the end.

> "The women said they could endure it . . . if, when all over, they could sleep off the terrible fatigue and for once drink all the pure sweet water they could desire. No more forced marches. No more gray road, stretching out its dusty miles as far as the eye could see."

Finally, as they entered the canyon Manly and Rogers had traversed to the Spanish ranch, ". . . we came to a little babbling brook. There it danced and jumped over the rocks singing the merriest songs one ever heard, as it said 'Drink, drink your fill ye thirsty one!' It was the happiest, sweetest music to the poor starved, thirsty souls, wasted down almost to haggard skeletons. O! If some poet of wildest imagination could only place himself in the position of those poor tired travelers to whom water in thick muddy pools had been a blessing, who had eagerly drunk the fluid even when so salt and bitter as to be repulsive, and now saw the clear, pure liquid, distilled from the crystal snow, abundant, free, filled with life and health—and could write in words the song of that joyous brook and set it to the music that it made as it echoed in gentle waves from the rocks and lofty walls!"

One can little blame Manly for his lyrically recalled memories. It was a sight that had tortured their dreams, that they despaired of ever coming true.

74

EPILOGUE

What happened to the '49ers who survived the valley of the shadow of death?

Many simply disappeared into the mainstream of life, never to be heard of again.

Despite his earlier intentions, Nusbaumer was never to "return home." As with many another forty-niner, the memories of the East were to pall in comparison with California's promised land.

Nusbaumer was to make his way from Los Angeles to San Francisco and mined on the Merced River throughout the summer of 1850. The following spring his beloved wife "Lisette", who made the trip via Panama, joined him. Although one scarcely needs help in picturing the joyous reunion, it is appropriate to record one of the supplemental entries to his journal, added in some of the little space left at the back:

> "There is no greater happiness in the world than being with one's family. A good faithful wife at his side and enough to be able to live decently is all that a man needs. I have now lost a year of my life since I had no one to whom I could attach myself. No one to whom I could open my heart and express my feelings. A year without love and joy. It is time lost."

With the exception of some eleven months in Oregon, Nusbaumer and his wife lived in San Francisco until the fall of 1856. They then moved to an 80 acre farm on Dry Creek in Washington township, in partnership with a C. Duerr. In October, 1857, Duerr and Nusbaumer leased the estate of a John W. Kottinger for a term of five years, where they engaged in merchandising and sheep raising. At the expiration of that lease they bought a joint interest in Rancho El Valle de San Jose, comprising about 3,000 acres.

On May 25, 1878, Lisette Nusbaumer died. It was a shock from which Louis never recovered and on July 10 of that same

A view of Los Angeles in 1853

year, at the age of 59, he reached the end of the trail, leaving four children—George, Albert, Emil and a daughter Bertha.

Of Hadapp, Schlogel and the Ehrhardts, nothing further is known. They may have kept in touch, at least now and then, by visits or letters, but there is no record. They may have gone to the "gold fields", turned farmers or city dwellers, or returned East or to the Old Country. Like shipboard friendships their camaraderie of the trail was intense at the time but apparently faded in the increasing tempo and distractions of life.

Manly, Rogers and the Bennetts arrived in Los Angeles after the Jayhawkers. Here Manly was hired by "Reverend" Brier who had started a boarding house in partnership with a Lewis Granger who had come through with Hunt's train. He was to haul water by ox-cart and to weed a vineyard for $50 a month plus a place to sleep atop a pile of old blankets in a small storeroom. Two weeks later, with half a month's pay in his pocket, Manly left to the north with a couple of horse buyers. Along the way he met Rogers and Bennett, continuing on with them to the gold country.

Manly had only fair results at mining. And at one of the mining camps sold the little one-eyed mule that had been so instrumental in saving the party in Death Valley and which he had fondly kept with him to this point.

A bit homesick and discouraged, Manly returned to his home in Wisconsin, via San Francisco and the Panama crossing. But as with many others who also returned, he found life "back home" less than what he had learned to love in California. So, in 1852 he returned, and understandably recalling the trials of traveling overland, he made this trip by boat— down the Mississippi to New Orleans, on to the Isthmus, and by ship to San Francisco and back to the mines!

In 1859 he turned to farming near San Jose, where he died on February 5, 1903, at the age of 83.

Rogers, Manly's close companion over the 1849-50 trail, settled in Merced, California. He, too, went mining and apparently also failed to strike it rich. Indicatively he went to work in a quicksilver (Mercury) mine or smelter, where the lethal fumes

77

gradually caused a loss of the use of his feet. In 1895, forty-one years since they last met, Manly found where Rogers was living and went to visit him. It was a touching reunion as they recalled their Death Valley days, and filled each other in on what had happened since.

Of the Arcanes little is known save that they parted from their other companions at the small ranch in San Fernando Valley, continuing to San Pedro and thence by ship to Santa Cruz, California.

After the death of his wife, Asabel Bennett went to Utah and remarried, to a Mormon girl. The last heard of Bennett was that he died in the Nevada mining town of Belmont,* about 100 miles from their trail of 1849 where they had seen the mirage that turned them southward.

The Wades, pausing only momentarily at Los Angeles, wended their way northward. First to a disappointing attempt at mining, then to farming, then freighting at a town called Alviso, at the southern tip of San Francisco Bay. In addition operated a hotel called "The American House", destroyed by fire in the 1860's. All the while he kept the wagon—the only wagon that survived the trek through Death Valley. Thirty years later it was still being used as a playhouse by his grandchildren. In a letter written by L. D. Stephens to fellow Jayhawker Colton there was an item that Henry Wade died a suicide at about 80 years of age.

The Briers eventually left Los Angeles to settle near Lodi, California. Lodi . . . Santa Cruz . . . San Jose . . . Merced, all of these lie within a close circle of each other. Whether so many of the '49ers gravitated to this area subconsciously seeking common bonds, or simply longing for greener scenery than they had experienced, is a matter of conjecture. Perhaps, too, as each attempted to find a fortune at mining, with less than notable results, they simply turned towards the dual attractions of the ocean—a wonder

---

*According to Death Valley '49er biographer John Ellenbecker, in his classic "The Jayhawkers of Death Valley." However, there is also a conflicting report that he died in Idaho, and that it is his son George who died in Belmont.

to many of them—and the facilities and settlements of the San Francisco Bay area.

In any event, it is interesting to note that small, slender Mrs. Brier died in 1913 at the age of 99 years, 8 months. Lest one view history as long-forgotten times, she had traveled by ox-drawn wagon yet lived to see the automobile and the airplane!

Indeed, the last of the Jayhawkers, L. Dow Stephens, died February 10, 1921!

For many years the Death Valley '49ers gathered at annual reunions. But one by one they slipped away. The last meeting attended by only two survivors, was in 1918.

Whatever their faults, whatever their failings, the members of the Death Valley Party of 1849 well deserve their honored niche in history. With little they overcame much. Inexperienced, oft illiterate, they seemed miscast for the heroic roles for which they were destined. They were tested as few have been called upon—and triumphed. They have provided us, and generations yet to come, with inspiration and pride in our great American heritage.

When you visit Death Valley, take the time to sit on the terrace of the modern lush Furnace Creek Inn. Look up the wash, easterly to Travertine Spring; north along the valley to where the Jayhawkers burned their wagons; and south to where those in the "Long Camp" endeavored to escape their valley of death. Then close your eyes, and listen—listen carefully for the soft, ever so soft desert winds to carry the time-faded sounds of strange men, in an even stranger and unknown land—the simmering expanse of Death Valley—of *Tomesha*—the land of "ground afire."

Other Death Valley '49er Inc. Publications

GEOLOGICAL STORY OF DEATH VALLEY
Dr. Thomas Clements

DEATH VALLEY TALES
by 10 noted authors

A NATURALIST'S DEATH VALLEY
Edmund C. Jaeger, Sc.D.

DEATH VALLEY & MANLY, SYMBOLS OF DESTINY
Ardis Manly Walker

GOODBYE, DEATH VALLEY!
L. Burr Belden

CAMELS AND SURVEYORS IN DEATH VALLEY
Arthur Woodward

FIFTY YEARS IN DEATH VALLEY
Harry Gower

DEATH VALLEY '49ERS COOKBOOK
Lydia Clements, Editor